HOLLY AND THE ROCK

by Sandy Dickson

**Illustrations by
Kevin Jones**

Copyright © 2019 Sandy Dickson
Copyright © 2019 TEACH Services, Inc.
ISBN-13: 978-1-4796-1003-7 (Paperback)
ISBN-13: 978-1-4796-1004-4 (ePub)
Library of Congress Control No: 2019934085

TEACH Services, Inc.
PUBLISHING
www.TEACHServices.com ● (800) 367-1844

Holly was excited about her trip to Israel and was anxious to learn all she could about the little country so rich with history.

Strolling through one of the streets, she wondered who might have walked the same streets before her. *How many of the very rocks and stones might have been stepped on by people who lived in the Bible days?* she wondered, but there was no way of knowing. She only knew they had been around for many years among some very interesting people. She thought about how wonderful it would be to have a chat with one of these rocks that had been a part of an ancient civilization.

As she looked at the many stones in the field near her, she wondered what they had seen in their many centuries of being there. Surely, they had some interesting stories.

She picked one up. It was gray and smooth; about the size of a fist and fit nicely into hers.

Playfully, she said, "Hello. I bet you have some fascinating things to tell if you could only talk."

"I do, and I can," it replied. "No one ever asked me before. What would you like to know?"

She was shocked. Was she hearing things? She looked at it sitting patiently in her hand. There was no one else around. "Yikes," she squealed and jerked her hand back quickly, dropping the rock to the ground. She looked around to see if anyone saw her talking to a rock.

"Ouch. That was a shock, but it didn't hurt too much. I'm used to abuse and being walked on. Now do you want to know something or what?" the rock said.

She walked to where it had fallen near her feet, and as a test, she asked, "How old are you?"

"As old as dirt," it replied.

She glanced around again. It was a bit embarrassing to be seen talking to a rock. But there was no one around, and the sound was definitely coming from the rock.

She slowly bent over and picked it up again, wrapping her fingers around it.

"Okay, that's better," it said. "Now what else do you want to know?"

"Well, if you're as old as dirt, we have a lot to talk about. What was it like to be around during the Bible days?"

"Do you mean the Old or New Testament days?"

"Let's start with the Old," she answered.

"Okay. Well, have a seat. I've got a lot to say."

"Do you mind if I call you Rock?"

"That sounds sensible to me," Rock said.

"All right, Rock. My name is Holly, and I'm so glad to meet you. Can you tell me some of your adventures through your time here?"

"Well, I remember being taken on the path from Egypt the Israelites took when Moses led them toward their promised land," Rock said. "I got kicked around often and moved by many feet and carts. I was also part of several loads of other rocks for different reasons when we were loaded into ox-drawn carts to be taken to different places, so I've traveled some. Someone picked me up on her way to the Red Sea to use as a weapon against the Egyptians if needed. She was shocked when the Red Sea waters parted. For a long time after we got to the other side, I rode inside a bag on a donkey.

"Some of the Israelites complained a lot about several things as the months went on, including the food. It was a lot of years before I wound up here in Israel, and by the time that happened, Joshua had become the leader, because Moses died."

"How fascinating!" Holly looked again at the rock in her hand. "You're a good-looking rock and a nice fist-size; easy to hold, but big enough to throw and do some damage."

"Yes, I can pack a wallop, and I think that's the reason I've gotten into so many adventures. My size is very good for lots of things. I've been dropped, but mostly thrown and picked up again by someone else, to be taken along as a handy weapon," Rock explained. "I've even spent some time in water, which is how I got so smooth. But I washed ashore and got picked up again."

"What else have you been part of that I might have heard about?"

"Okay. Joseph walked over me with his brothers when I was in the land of Canaan, and they were on their way to dump him in that well. Then years later when they went to Egypt to buy food during the famine, I saw them again. One of them stepped right on me."

"Do you feel important?" Holly asked.

"No, I'm just a rock—one of many God made, but no more important than any other one. We all have our purpose. There is one very important one, though."

"Do you have other rock friends?"

"Sure, I know a lot of other rocks; of course, I come from a very large family. Some I don't see often, others I spend a lot of time being next to until one of us gets shifted around for some reason, by someone or something. I move a little around here, but not much. My location changes a bit with livestock or people, especially in wars when there's a lot of activity around me. I haven't been moved to a faraway location for quite a while now; a few centuries at least, so I know those in this neighborhood pretty well."

"If I carry you around Israel to other places, can you introduce me to some other rocks?" Holly asked excitedly.

"Sure, I wouldn't mind traveling some again," he answered cheerfully. "I don't like being in one place all the time, and I haven't gone anywhere at all in at least several eons, except being kicked around by a few sheep."

"All right, I'm going to carry you in my pocket between places for now. Is that okay?"

"I think so, although I'm not too sure what a pocket is."

"They probably didn't have pockets in the Bible days when you were last carried by a person, but I'll show you."

With that, Holly put Rock in her pocket and moved on, saying aloud, "When I get somewhere else with other rocks that look interesting, I'll let you know."

Rock later told her that it felt snug and warm against the soft material of the pocket lining, finding it quite comfortable and agreeable.

A few miles later, Holly pulled the rock out again. "Do you recognize any of this?" she asked.

"Yes," it said. "This is where someone picked me up and used me to throw at someone during a stoning. I hit the man right in the ankle and made him limp around for a while. It made a loud noise when I hit. I was good for that sort of thing. I'm afraid I've been used in several of those stonings. It was very popular back then. Some of those huge rocks like that one over there are why I remember this place. They are too big to move, so they got off lucky. They were never used to hurt anyone, but then they never had any adventure either. They've been in one place because people can't pick them up. But there's one rock that's more important than any other; that is bigger than all the rest, yet you can't see that one."

"That sounds like a riddle. How can it be so big and important that no one can see it?" Holly wondered aloud.

"I'll tell you, but not now. First, I want to see some more things. These are good memories for me," Rock said. "I'm having a good time."

Sometimes Holly kept the rock in her pocket for several hours, sometimes for days, but it said it didn't mind the darkness because it was used to being outside all the time and there are many hours of darkness there, just as there are many hours of light. Rock was just glad to be traveling.

Once when they were in a particular location, Holly pulled the rock out again, and it started talking.

"Oh, that big rock over there is a famous hiding place from enemies during battle. Hey, walk over closer to that smaller rock beneath it," Rock said. "Now take me around that tree. Okay, that's what I thought. I recognize the landmarks. See that little rock about my size next by the bigger brown rock? Put me down beside it for a minute. I want to check it out."

When Holly did so, Rock said to the other rock, "Well, hello, how are you doing? I haven't seen you since long ago. Have you been around here all this time?"

"Yeah," it said. "I don't get around much being way out here where there's not much foot traffic, although I've been kicked around through a few battles. It's okay, though. I like it here."

Rock said to Holly, "This is a very important rock," then to the rock, "Tell her what you did."

"Oh, you mean that one battle with the giant?"

"Yes, that one."

"Okay. Well, there was an encampment of soldiers up on the hill, and a kid came along and put me in his sling. He slung me around a few times and let me go sailing through the air. God guided me, and next I knew—plunk. I landed right in the middle of someone's forehead with a loud cracking noise. This big giant named Goliath fell to the ground, and the ground shook. I killed him, and I'm sure God guided me! Everyone was pretty excited about it. And here I sit, still in the same general location."

"That's one of the most popular stories in the Bible," Holly said excitedly. "It's amazing that I got to meet you. I bet no one knows who you are."

"No one could," it said. "There are lots of us that have done some pretty important things through time, like the rock where Jacob laid his head when he had the dream about Heaven's ladder, but no one could ever possibly know. We just sit here all over, people walk around us and on us and have no idea, but we don't care. We've been created for a purpose, we fulfill it, and that's just how it is. We weren't created for our own glory or to be recognized."

"Well, I'm certainly honored to meet you," Holly assured it.

Holly was surprised at the wonderful things that no one ever sees or knows, as they walked around the streets of Jerusalem and saw the same holy and famous places where the Old and New Testament people walked.

Holly met rocks that David had rested upon during his years of running from Saul. Some larger ones even gave David shelter because they were always there and dependable.

Rock said, "We smaller rocks might be all right for some things temporarily, but we change location occasionally, and we're not always around when people need us. Not only that, but the big ones serve as landmarks and often guide the way. I'd never have found that Goliath rock for you if it hadn't been for larger ones I saw to guide me there. And by the biggest rock I've been talking about that you can't see, you can always find your way, too."

Holly understood what Rock meant and began to see rocks in a whole new way. The big rocks stay in the same place and have seen all kinds of awesome and well-known Biblical events, such as when the chariot of fire whisked Elijah away to the heavens and many others that were in both Old and New Testament stories. Holly marveled at how exciting it was that so many of them were still around, though no one could possibly know as they walk those age-old and well-traveled streets and pass the ancient fields.

There were even rocks still sitting around that the angels had flung at enemies of God's children.

"There is still that rock that is bigger and higher than all others," Rock said. "It serves as a refuge and tower of strength—a shelter that you can dwell inside, even if you can't see it," he added. She could tell he was enjoying this confusing description.

The most heart-stopping rocks to her so far had stories to tell about Jesus, such as those that were present at varied locations to see His healings or turn small amounts of fish and bread into enough to feed thousands. She especially was excited to see the one who had said Jesus had walked on it while carrying the cross to Calvary. But she was very curious about this bigger rock and figured it must be a mountain; yet how could a mountain not be seen?

When Rock introduced her to the rock Jesus had actually stepped on, on His way to Calvary, she said to that one, "I'm amazed that you experienced that huge and important event. What did it feel like?" she added, thinking that was a stupid question.

Surprisingly, it said, "It felt extremely heavy. Much more so than anything I had ever experienced when anyone else walked over me, or even when a cart drove over me, and they had been doing that for centuries."

"Why was that?" Holly asked. "How could Jesus be heavier than those other things? He wasn't a large man, was He? Of course, He was carrying that big cross."

"No, He wasn't large and yes, He was carrying the cross," that rock said. "But He was carrying much more than that. He was carrying the weight of all the sins of the world and all the future sins that would ever be committed, too. It was an immense burden."

With this thought, tears sprang to Holly's eyes. The description allowed her to picture Christ's struggle in her mind very clearly and realize what a painful sacrifice He had made for all humanity.

When she was finally able to speak, she said, "Okay, Rock, this has been more fabulous than I could ever imagine. But now where is that rock that is so huge that I can never see it?"

"Oh, *that* rock—the biggest rock that will ever be. That's Jesus. He's called 'The Rock' because He's always there, even if people can't see Him. He's a rock-solid refuge, Comforter, and Protector. He's the Son of God. He's like some of those rocks you saw that don't move and never change, like the rocks to which David fled for rest and safety from his problems and the soldiers chasing him. The big rocks were always there, and David knew where and how to find them.

"Jesus is not going anywhere. He's a Rock too big to cast aside or misplace, and He's dependable. You can always go to Jesus when you want to because you know where to find Him. I heard Jesus say, 'Seek, and you shall find.' He said, 'I am the way, the truth, and the life.' He's a dependable guide, always findable and just a prayer away. He is the Rock of salvation and even spiritual refreshment. The large rocks can guide the way as landmarks as they did for me.

"Jesus does the same. He's the biggest rock of all for any who want to find shelter, comfort, or guidance for the right way. There are small, unimportant things like us smaller rocks, which can even be a temporary comfort to people for one reason or another. Therefore, we do have and serve a purpose, but we're only temporary and can't always be found in the same place. Sometimes we can't even be found at all when someone needs us. Rocks don't come to you when you need them; you have to look for them. It's much like having to look for Jesus because God gave man freedom of choice. Jesus, of course, can come to people, but He usually prefers to wait for an invitation. In that way, He knows it's sincere."

In her imagination, Holly saw again that precious Man: Jesus, the Son of God who came to earth, walking so painfully on that path to Calvary under the massive burden of all sin—even those yet to happen throughout time—for those who believe in Him, so that, because of His journey and death, they could have everlasting life in Heaven with Him and all other believers who have lived before them. Yes indeed, Jesus *is* the biggest Rock!

TEACH Services, Inc.
P U B L I S H I N G
www.TEACHServices.com ● (800) 367-1844

We invite you to view the complete
selection of titles we publish at:
www.TEACHServices.com

We encourage you to write us
with your thoughts about this,
or any other book we publish at:
info@TEACHServices.com

TEACH Services' titles may be purchased in
bulk quantities for educational, fund-raising,
business, or promotional use.
bulksales@TEACHServices.com

Finally, if you are interested in seeing
your own book in print, please contact us at:
publishing@TEACHServices.com

We are happy to review your manuscript at no charge.

www.ingramcontent.com/pod-product-compliance
Lightning Source LLC
Chambersburg PA
CBHW061416090426
42742CB00026B/3487